A Sense of My Dream, Goal, and the Success

Where and how it all began

Dr. Chris Inyang

Printed in the United States of America

ISBN: Softcover   978-1-63871-529-0
       Hardcover   978-1-63871-531-3
       eBook   978-1-63871-530-6

Republished by: PageTurner Press and Media LLC
Publication Date: 09/02/2021

To order copies of this book, contact:

PageTurner Press and Media
Phone: 1-888-447-9651
info@pageturner.us
www.pageturner.us

Contents

Acknowledgment

Writing this bio befitted mandatory to communicate to the world that impossibility can become conceivable if a person works firm to obtain it. In this case, I did, and the outcome was immense. Therefore, I articulate this 'wow' to myself that I had crossed many rivers to reach my destination when my enemies weren't sure I would. This success couldn't turn into reality without the support of my family. They stood with me to the finished line, which brought the feeling of saying 'wow' am proud and honored to stay alive and witness this moment of happiness. Folks, never give up in life, keep the hope alive as your turn is getting closer than you ever think, and what you need to do is to progress on and not recoil as Gods' time profess is the best time.

Introduction

As the author of this autobiography, I, Dr. Chris Inyang (Dr. I), would like to explain a sense of my dream, goal, and success. Indeed, this dream occurred decades ago when I was a teenage boy. This dream allowed me to recognize the importance and viability that played in my life and has encouraged and bequeathed a sense of urgency to trail the path of education. The dream linked to my success in life, which I took time to analyze, planned, and implemented. I get it that an individual dream can become a reality or deceptive at times, depending on how one analyzes and interprets them. I understood that a vision sometimes appears as images, ideas, emotions, and sensations that occur involuntarily in the minds during a particular stage of one's sleep. To this day, this dream continues to guide and direct my affairs in life.

I had numerous dreams whose meanings I couldn't explain. However, at the earliest stage, whenever I dreamed, the inclination, I sensed suggested an inevitable on the way coming. For what purpose, to whom, where and what date became a total misery to which I couldn't lay my hand on any. Unequivocally, most time when I felt a strange sign on the left hand or leg, I interpreted it as a sign of evil. On the other hand, if a sensation occurred in the right hand or leg, an indication of a valued news. These dreams of mine usually come in the form of an event, family members, relatives, friends, or even a distant person. The vision on the number of occasions, reflected extraordinary things which I had executed, such as helping others to achieve their objectives and fighting against human injustice. The benevolent spirit pleased me, as I could rescue people in my dream. The idea of helping further emboldens my wish to work hard in the education and I wanted the alleged dreams to appear in its realism. Notably, I had never doubted or been 99.9 percent satisfied with the visions, and therefore, I seek several consultations with the people, including my mother.

I received others enormous advice that signified a sign of courage, a brighter future, and dignity. As for my mother's advice, she specifically advised that no matter what, I should stay focused in school. Convincingly enough, I was excited and pleased with the useful answers and the supported ideas every person had contributed. My approach in handling issues since the advice has changed significantly to normal; therefore, in that note, I decided to occupy myself with doing more reasonable things, such as reading different books, hanging with impeccable friends who can offer great ideas. As a result of the advice and words of wisdom, my long waiting with the positive attitude and focus has granted me the hope for the future, and I would become the first graduate in my family.

I quickly recognized my need to pursue education, which I believed represents the highest achievement I can get. I visualized education to stand as a stream of my hope. Though, before I embarked on the journey, I reminded of myself the dynamics that involved in my dreams. I simply asked myself what purpose I would wish to prepare. The answer was pointed at education, where I desired to build myself in the areas of human capital, broaden perspective, improve potential, find better job prospects, and dispose inequality. Over the years, I had witnessed quite a significant number of people with education, the valuable contribution to people's lives, particularly in my life; I have become a responsible citizen. From education, I understood my history and culture, and I had absorbed its values. Seemingly, education has opened many minds, including mine, and expands many horizons. The value of education enables me in the society to understand my duties as a citizen and encourages the education. I chose the path to education to maintain a status symbol and stick to its ideals for the rest of my life. The pathway to life had revolved around education. There is no denying that anywhere in the world, an educated person is a better citizen. In this premise, my dream has been much directed toward a goal setting in life, which, below, I explained the steps of encouragement from my dream.

The Steps of Encouragement from My Dream

Making my dreams come truly makes my life very motivating and exciting. The simple act of dreaming arouses the dreams and injects importance and purpose to my life. When I cease dreaming, I depart for heaven. When I hold on to dreams, I am grasping at my life. I am always daydreaming, and my daydreams make my future. But if my daydreams are cataleptic and purposeless, then I make an incubus for my future. And when I am carefully planning my daydreams through the process of visualization, I make a dreamy, magical future. Dreams affect life, adding exciting prospects of even the dullest of days. If I don't dream about the future, how will I know where I am going? When I foster my dreams, my dreams foster me. The more I can dream, the more I can do.

With respect to the goal setting, this is another crucial characteristic that demands my accountability. This is potent and doable, however, and difficult to engross. Apparently, I didn't care how difficult it might be. All that I wanted was the desired result, one that I could envision, plan, and commit to achieving the objective. This was my personal wish, an end point, and an expected development. Pragmatically, I wasn't sure how I can handle the situation, nevertheless, more appreciatively, from a friend who had a similar case. He taught me how difficult it was to implement and affect a goal setting due to various reasons. According to him, in order for me to be successful in a goal setting, it requires diligent planning to achieve the best outcome. The suggestion was agreed and added to the fact that a goal setting builds a virtuous motivator in both performance and focus. This helped create a commitment and drive plans and feedback. Therefore, these ideas permit my endeavors to reach within a finite time placed by a deadline.

After the positive aspiration and burning desire for my needs, I had carefully planned to become a successful person in life. I knew of a friend who didn't plan well; he confided that he felt adrift in the world of calamity. He claimed to have worked hard enough in his life, although he couldn't seem to get anywhere worthwhile. There was much to learn from his mistakes; however, I pushed ahead in my goal setting. Irrespective of the dilemma my friend and others were involved in, I recognized that things were not what it was, especially when it came to understanding what it meant to achieve the education in today's competitive world. I drew the conclusion that it didn't matter if Mr. A was failing or if Mr. B would be successful. In that regard, I implied Mr. A's failure was a self-made issue and lack of a cohesive planning or spending enough quality time in studying his homework. Also, it appeared that Mr. A didn't set himself up to a formal goal. My goal setting was basically a key factor and ideal future that motivated my vision that brought reality. Setting a goal had helped me tremendously by providing a road map, clarified my thinking, helped prepare for obstacles before it occurs, generated enthusiasm, and gave a sense of purpose. In another way of putting, the process helped choose a destination I had always wanted in life. Most importantly, I was conversant with what I wanted to do and where I had in mind to concentrate my efforts.

I planned my goal setting with full consciousness. In other words, it was my conscious decision to create. The big picture that envisaged a goal setting emanated from my dream. The short-term plan wasn't an option for me; however, I wanted the long-term goal. The planning and execution process took about twenty three and a half year. The breakdown was as follows: six years in the elementary school, five years in the secondary school, four years in the undergraduate, two and a half of the master's program, and six years in the doctoral degree program. During the days in school, I stayed focused until the last day. There were no worries for the fact I didn't have any person to help pay my tuitions, buy books, or help in any capacity. Only my mother helped in the primary school. After her death, the rest of my quest lingered solely in my head. With that, there was no sign of worries, neither did I ever fringe or think of giving up on life; there wasn't a father, a mother, relatives, or someone to come to my rescue. In all my engagements, I took a joy in supporting me by any possible means I can. Quite a significant number of people confronted the similar issue with each day passing by, and literally, they endured the pains and passed through the storming waters. By watching these people survive, it sufficed to say that I would duplicate the same.

Before I embarked on the journey, I predicted a tough road ahead. Indeed, I walked through it and turned impossibility to possibility. My goal-setting plan was focused until the end. It translated into a good success in my life.

What is success? Success, by definition, is an achievement of one's goal, they anticipated outcome of an attempt, or one that has already been prosperous. Let me try a different way. It's like soccer, basketball, and baseball establishments that made many folks understand success as almighty money, fame, and power, but there are abundant tales of unfulfilled lives and burnout among the so-called successful folks who indicated otherwise. Success is not an exclusive accomplishment or properties. Therefore, my success represents audaciousness of my hope. This signified the importance for both my personal and professional life in a significant number of ways. In the society, the highest-paid people are those that know more than the average ones. The people with education tend to understand the critical facts and information than an average person in the field.

These categories of educated ones can make more valuable contributions to a knowledge-based society and the best life possible. These people also are valued, respected, and eventually paid substantial money and promoted regularly. The ideas came to me as the inspirational motivation to take a path of education to earn more and increase the level of income and make a life, increase the level of intellectual capital and, thus, the value of the knowledge element of what I was exploiting.

By successfully completing my educational goal, I stand fit to handle any situation that comes my way. This introductory page of the efficacy of a sense of my dream, goal, and the success enumerated a step by-step occurrence during my life longevity. Finally, before I delve into more discussions in the following chapters, it's imperative to indicate here that I have a drive and commitment to learning and applying information, ideas, theories, and formulas to make a variety of tasks and goals in my life.

Important Note:! Being successful in life is not only if you have or not a parent, uncles, relatives, and good Samaritans; however, it also only necessitates when you put your effort, zeal, tenacity, and hard work!

CHAPTER 1

MY EARLY LIFE AND LESSONS LEARNED

I was formally named Mr. Christopher Hanson Inyang. People called me in my native name as (Akpan Uwan Ekan or Obong-Owo), meaning chief in the English translation, the name of my grandfather. I was born in 1960 and raised in Atanuk, in Mkpat Enin local government area, Akwa Ibom, Nigeria, from Ibibio tribe, with an Efik-speaking dialect. I have a polygamous background and a father with wealth and influence in his own inalienable right. A passionate and powerful person in nature, he loves the engagement in the farming business. My father was a devoted Christian fellow with impeccable records, the founder of Zion Church who was deeply involved in the church activities. He had three different wives with ten children. The following are the breakdown among the children: four were from the first marriage, another four were from the second marriage, and the last two came from the third marriage. Everyone in the family fully supported him. The entire family also stood behind him and fought no matter what during the farming season, their business, the main generated income for the family.

My father was not an educated person, nor was any of his family members. The understanding of the education was inconsequential to him. Therefore, it became the reason seven of his children, both boys and girls, never in their lifetime attended school. To my father, it was a cultural phenomenon; other families in the village and the surroundings thought the same. The people weren't keen on sending their children to school; however, what interested them most was the domestic duties. The girls in their early ages engaged in marriages. Only the oldest son of the family had a primary school education; nevertheless, he didn't complete it. The man took the interest in being a motor mechanic. My sister and I, from the second marriage, were the lucky ones to have attended and finished a primary school education, through the effort of our mother. This happened after the demise of my father. My father and I didn't understand each other well; I was still a young man during the time. To be fair with my father, I never confirmed with him if he would or couldn't have sponsored my sister and me through school if he was still living.

My Interest and Activities

I was the only surviving male child of my mother, an exclusive beneficiary of my mother's and sister's attention, for better or worse. My personality, however, added immensely to plenty of the fundamental life lessons I learned from my parents nurtured in Atanuk, from people from nearby villages, from relatives on the mother's side, from boys and girls in the surrounding area, through sports in school and other social means. I went to Atanuk primary school. The school had only primary 1, 2, and 3. In primary 4, 5, and 6, I continued at the Ikot Ekong Primary School. Atanuk was just a stone's throw from Ikot Ekong. In 1971, I completed my primary school education. During the days in the primary school, I became a servant to three different teachers. I also served a man who lived in my village temporarily due to the house-construction business he had. At school, I discovered the premium I enlisted on winning a game I executed, and on the flip side, the depraved taste left in my mouth happened when I lost a game or anything dear to my person. The athletics were my hobbies—in particular, soccer, one-hundred-meter dash, and relay races. I joined the groups of the (Ekpo-Nyoho, Ekpo-Ntuk-Odio-Dio, Ekon) masquerade dance. These groups were very popular in the area. At many times, I traveled out to perform at the special event, and I usually received payment for the service rendered. These traditional masquerade dance groups became popular mostly in the Christmas time and the official events. In school, I wasn't an 'A' one student; however, in sports, I become the indisputable champion. There was plenty of love in my person, especially for girls; I was a star and icon to them.

The people gave a protection, and they handled my person like an egg. My school was included on the state map, with the impeccable records of achievements. Severally, people regarded my talent as God-given. I was a centerpiece in my school and others. Everyone in my school was pleased with my records and the awards I received. The ability and ingenuity prompted other surrounding schools to come and seek for my service. Whenever they sought, I responded with kindness, and I was pleased to join and play in their game and win. There were constant requests for the assistance. In most of the games I participated, they awarded me with money, and they accommodated and fed me through the entire periods I remained with them. I never disappointed anyone. I gave my best performance, and most of the time, I came out victorious. My brilliant performances in the sports merited or identified my person as a champion.

Despite involvement in the sports activities, my one eye was still focused solely on making money in the business venture. As a village breed, I watched my elders make their traditional native baskets (ikat), sleeping mats (*ikan*), native bags (*nkon ayia*), traps for hunting (*afia ikot*), and fish traps and sold the items on the market. These kinds of skills became the main occupation for young people in the village. Apparently, I was in love, and I learned the business methods; it remained the only source of income. Buying and selling of provisions also coexisted, such as kerosene, cigarette, and pure water. The selling of these items generated enough income for my upkeep, and I was able to buy items needed in schools such as shoes, clothes, and many more. The trap business was for the personal consumption. The business kept my life afloat with my pocket full of money. Conversely, I never bothered my mother for money. Besides, I helped other people, including my junior sister. The items sold in the market were only once a week. The market days rotated, held on any day of the week, Monday through Saturday. If the market held on Monday through Friday, I could only attend after the school hours. When I went, I always brought some items back for resale in the village. This was a repeated event in every market day.

I never lack anything, and during the holiday time, I visited relatives of my choice and spent some time with them before going back to the village. I really loved holiday periods for six consecutive years. When I visited, they usually bought me some gifts. At times, my friends and I would travel to the main fishing village, where I made some money before my classes resume. I stayed for about three to four weeks and made enough money for my needs. For the six years in the primary school, I traveled to several places to meet both new and old friends. I also visited other interesting places. My character caused some people to label my person as a stubborn fellow. There was never a time I had withdrawn from a fight when someone looked for one. It didn't matter how big or tall the person was. I never allowed anyone to talk me down in any kind of way. With my headaches, it became a devastated blow to my mother. Indeed, I was a stubborn guy in the family. Perhaps I didn't have someone to check on my excesses. Because of that, she couldn't control me. Severally, many people in the village came to report one evil thing I had committed after another to my mother. To fight was most commonly a trademark, I should say; it didn't matter whether the person was a male or female. My fighting habit had led to more troubles, mostly with the female counterparts. One day, in a fight, a female friend struck a bottle on the back of my head. As a result, I became unconscious for three to four hours at the scene. When she realized that I was a vegetable, she ran away without waiting to see my health condition, for fear of being lynched by my village boys. After a few days, I gained back my consciousness. My mind was telling to reiterate the assault meted out on my person; however, friends said the plan shouldn't go forward with the intent.

My inexplicable manners were not visible or showed after my primary school graduation. I guess I was a grown-up man. Basically, I focused toward entering college with my colleagues. Although I knew my plan required money for the project, I still went ahead to obtain an admission form, filled it out, and submitted it. In December 1971, initially, I didn't disclose this plan to anybody except my closest friends. I wanted to take everyone by surprise. I notified my elder stepbrother, whom I regarded as a father to me, and the head of the family to support my cause in going to the secondary school. He was based in Port Harcourt at a time, the Rivers State Capital. He worked for Shell Petroleum Company, and money wasn't an issue. From the conversation we had, he indicated the readiness to take the challenge. To the point, that meant my going school was certain. It was at the last stage that I decided confide in my mother about the secret plan. I also broke news about my elder brother's willingness to sponsor my education, but she was doubtful of such gesture from him. She stipulated that the idea was just a daydream. She explained that he hadn't supported anybody in his entire life, so how would he want to take this huge responsibility this time? Obviously, she told me that she didn't want to get herself involve in a project that she wouldn't get to finish if he decided to back out. Also, she said she couldn't afford to support two people in school at the same time. She was referring to my junior sister and me. Her message was clearer and louder for me. I didn't blame her at all because she was telling the whole truth. After two weeks,

the result of the common entrance examination came out, and I passed it. Following the result was an admission letter, which I was very excited about, ready to proceed to the school. The school started in January of 1973, and every arrangement was made and completed, but I waited, and I didn't hear from my brother, nor did I receive any money. It was after a couple of weeks that passed by that I realized my going to school wasn't going to happen and that my mother rightly warned me about school sponsorship by my brother. I wasn't happy with the development, but there was nothing I could have done to prevent the shameful treatment I received. I waited a couple of weeks to decide my next line of action, so I left everything in God's hands to direct my vision.

In December of 1972, at Christmas season, when many people returned to the village to celebrate with their loved ones, was the same year my stepsister visited home from Lagos, where she resided with her immediate family, including her husband. In the evening of that faithful Friday, the twentieth day in December, the news, filtered town that my stepsister was in her husband's village. I didn't go to see her immediately, but I waited for her to come to greet us in our village (Atanuk), her birthplace as the tradition demands. Sure, she came down to the family, and every member of the family celebrated with her. I didn't know my mother had some discussions with her about me going away from the village to Lagos for a change. My mother told me that she agreed to her proposal. The news broke after she had left back to her husband's village. I was

very excited and happy about the development. The news went to town; my friends were happy to hear that, and they wished me the best of luck in Lagos. Also, some friends weren't happy because I was leaving them behind. My mother was very excited and pleased for the fact that I was leaving for good. Before my departure, she gathered some foodstuff to take with me. She gave me a transport fare. In January 1973, the journey to Lagos had begun, where a new chapter would be written.

CHAPTER 2

FIRST TRANSITION

Atanuk to Lagos

In January 1973, I left Atanuk to uncharted territory (Lagos). This was a good portent on my part, a place I hadn't visited before. Initially, when I arrived, I was bored, but quickly I dismissed the feeling; I was just a few weeks in town. I realized that I was in Lagos and not my village. I knew from the onset my stay in Lagos wasn't going to be pretty for some time to come. So I stuck to my mother's advice that stated that I shouldn't be afraid of anything that came my way but stay focused and aim. The message was louder and clearer. I forced myself to heed my mother's advice.

With less time in my hand, I quickly adjusted to the normal life. Since then, I have had a freedom of movement, such as going to the market and stores, meeting friends, and many others. Along the way, I made both new and old friends. There was a village boy I met in Lagos who came two weeks before me; he couldn't cope with the life in Lagos, so he decided to go back to the village and settle down there. I didn't want to take his footstep; I stayed. I started my first job at the Federal Public Service Commission as a messenger. The job didn't last long enough because of my constant lateness to work. As a novice in Lagos, I didn't understand the procedure working for the government or any company. My job terminated, and I felt bad about it, but life must continue. I learned a lesson after I lost my first job. It didn't take me a long time to secure another job through a contract from the National Electric Power

Authority (NEPA). I worked directly for a contractor. The job was part-time, Saturdays and Sundays. The job description was to supervise others. The work was to place electric cables on the ground in different sites in Lagos metropolitan areas and the surroundings. I made a lot of money, and I also spent it carelessly sometimes. I helped my mother in the village, and I contributed to the house I was living in Lagos.

It was an abrupt stay with my in-laws. I left them and rented my own apartment. I lived alone, and I kept a girlfriend, who was a well-mannered person. I was an addict to card playing for money. I had many friends who played cards as well. My apartment turned into a center for playing cards. All sorts of manners were shown among my friends. A lot of time, people fought, especially when a person lost money on card playing. I lent money to friends, and they looked at me as a good person. I shared my history with them. They understood that I never get defeated in a fight. I protected my friends, and they protected me too. Because of the good things I had done for my friends, they respected and named me the *Mighty Igor*. Everybody in the neighborhood called and addressed me by the name. I was benevolent to everyone in my clique. I had many friends, and, I had many enemies. I had two assassination attempts in Lagos; the first attempt was connected to a girlfriend who befriended another guy before me. The guy thought I snatched the girl away from him. They knew each other from primary school days. The second attempt was when I tried to help a friend recover his money from another person. In both incidents, I was hospitalized for about two to three weeks.

I visited my village during my vacation period. Usually, at Christmastime, when I visited, I stayed three or four weeks before I returned to Lagos. I joined a NEPA Football Club, the Islanders, a division 3 football club in Lagos Island and beyond. I played in many of the league tournaments. I attended a commercial institute to learn how to type, write shorthand, among others in 1973. In 1974, I attended a full-time community high school, where I prepared for my West African School Certificate (WASC). I also attended Christ Church Cathedral School Center to prepare for the November/December General Certificate of Education (GCE). In 1974 to 1982, I bagged my first diploma from the Pitman Examination Council in London in typing of twenty-five and thirty-five words per minute. I also grabbed, between 1979 and 1982, another diploma in both GCE/WASC, respectively. In 1981, I stopped working.

A part-time job and engaged in a full-time permanent job with NEPA. I started as a cable jointer's mate and stayed a short time in the position. Later, I switched to become a dispatch operator. Again, I saw another switch; this time, it was as a secretary in the investigation department and, finally later transferred, to represent the Ikoyi NEPA branch office. I worked diligently throughout the periods with the National Electric Power Authority (NEPA).

While in the Ikoyi office, I made many friends. I tried to obtain an American visiting visa, but I failed. I even paid someone to help, but still, it didn't work. I decided to go through Yugoslavia after I had made five attempts on five different passports to secure an American visa, but all failed. Right from the beginning, I had wanted to come to America to study. I fell in love with the Americans, especially with the way they speak, their culture, and many more. There were few Youth Corpers in my school, and they studied in America. I liked their lifestyles. They usually stayed in groups during lunchtime and chatted together in an American accent. I loved it, and I wished I could speak like them. These guys took over our girls because they came from America. They drove nice cars with American plate numbers on them. Their behaviors were quite different from ours. After all that, I planned to leave for Yugoslavia. I met and established a cordial relationship with a diplomat friend from the Yugoslavian embassy in Lagos. I took six months to prepare for the journey. I didn't tell anybody about my plan until the last two weeks of the departure. I intimated with my in-laws and some close associates before heading to the village to tell my mother and others. I broke the news, and there was a lot of joy. I received the blessing from everyone, and I returned to Lagos. In Lagos, friends organized a farewell party in my honor.

CHAPTER 3
SECOND TRANSITION

Lagos to Yugoslavia

In March of 1983, I arrived in Yugoslavia safely, a different country from Nigeria. I didn't have any knowledge of the environment or anyone or knew what my expectations were. The people were friendly; however, the language proved difficult to comprehend. Fewer people spoke English. On my arrival, I became confused; thus, I couldn't communicate in the language, though I did communicate with the taxi cab driver to take me to the student hostel. Luckily, at the hostel, I found a fellow Nigerian student that came to my aid. Very helpful and accommodating, the fellow accepted to provide me accommodation for a few days until he could find me a place where I could stay. This gentleman did his best and made sure I was comfortable. I learned many things from him, particularly the people and the city life. Other Nigerians played a crucial role, and I learned quite significantly from them too. After a couple of days, I signed up for language course I and II. The language course lasted for nine-month periods (Serbian language), and it commenced in March through November 1983. Before I started my university course, I enrolled in sports and other social activities. At the student service center, I took a job working in the factory as a laborer. In November of 1983 after my language course, I completed the paperwork to start my course in the political science faculty at the University of Belgrade. The course was scheduled to last for four years and offered a BA degree in political science. The study was progressing.

In 1984, I enlisted as a secretary-general for the Nigerian Student Union, Belgrade, to represent the entire Nigerian students in Yugoslavia. As a student, life looked difficult to cope with; money became the major issue. A friend introduced to me a way of making legal money to survive while in school. The business involved traveling out to different parts of Europe in search of summer holiday jobs and buying and selling items in Belgrade. This became popular and lucrative for most us foreigners. However, I engaged in the business, and I made enough money to sustain me for few months. From the proceeds, I could help my friends. As a foreigner, I had the liberty and freedom to travel to anywhere I desired. The problem I usually had emanated from the Yugoslav/ Italian custom and police officials at the border with their constant harassment. They usually searched, and if found with contraband items, I was dropped off at the border and asked to return those items back to Italy, where I bought them before coming back into the country. Other times, they seized every item and locked me up in the cell for a day or two. The people didn't grasp what to do with me or the other foreigners. We survived with the business being the only means of making money. My quick release at times depended on the officer's mood. In 1984/1985, I invited my nephew (A. A. Alexander) into Yugoslavia. I created a transitional way for him in the country. Since I helped him, he registered in the language course. Through effort, he gained admission to the advanced school of studies. Within a short stay together, I left him to continue my third year in the University of Zagreb, Department of Political Science. I completed my first- and second-year studies in Belgrade.

CHAPTER 4
THIRD TRANSITION

Zagreb to America

I took another interesting journey from Zagreb to America. After several failed attempts at procuring a visa in Nigeria, the American embassy in Zagreb enhanced the issuance of a visa. The visa was valid for a three-month stay in America. During my time in Zagreb, I remained a final-year student at the University of Zagreb. I prepared for the interview at the American embassy. Several questions were asked, including why I needed to visit the United States of America, whom I wanted to visit, and where the person resided. To avoid implicating or complicating my chances of visiting America, I simply answered that I wanted to visit the Statue of Liberty in New York City and the nation's capital, Washington, DC. I refused to mention names in the USA. I didn't travel on the first issued visa. I let it expire for the lack of money. I went back a second time for a reissue for another three months. I succeeded, and my friends applauded my effort. However, I didn't have money for the airline ticket, so I decided to take a quick job in the student service center to raise funds. It worked out well for a couple of weeks, and I made the money for the airline ticket.

Still, with the little money, I had only bought a few items, which were not enough, so I took a trip to Nigeria to raise more funds. When leaving for Nigeria, I bought a few items to sell. I sold them and added the money to remit back to Zagreb, Yugoslavia. I used that opportunity to confer with my people about my next line of action, which meant my desire not to come back home to seek for an employment, which I promised after my graduation at the University of Zagreb. I confer with them about my plan to travel to America for further studies. According to them, it was a brilliant idea and a good move on my part. They congratulated my effort in successfully completing the first degree. They wished me a safe journey back to Zagreb and then to America. I came back to Zagreb and only had a week left to travel to the United States of America. I used the entire one week to gather the items I needed, including the buying and booking of the airline ticket.

I wanted to leave on December 21, 1988, from Zagreb to connect with a Pan Am Flight 103 in London to the USA. Thank God, I didn't travel on the airline as initially planned. Later on, that day, it was reported in the news that the Pan Am Flight 103 exploded at 31,000 feet over Lockerbie, Scotland, 38 minutes after takeoff, killing all 259 passengers and crew members, along with 11 people on the ground. On February 9, 1989, I left Zagreb through Amsterdam (Holland) to New York (USA). Before I left for the USA, I had two friends there: Mr. Udo Cox in Atlanta, Georgia, and Mr. Charles Alatise in Baltimore, Maryland (USA). Both men were students in Yugoslavia before they had an opportunity for America. Mr. Alatise lived in Novi Sad in Belgrade, while Mr. Cox and I lived in Zagreb. Through my effort, Alatise obtained an America visiting visa. These two friends left for America before me. None of them had any idea about my coming to the USA. Mr. Udo came to America a year ahead of me (he lived with his uncle), while Mr. Alatise came a few months ahead of me. However, I decided to take my own risk. I didn't understand where I would stay when I arrived. God became the only hope to direct my affairs while in the USA. I landed safely in New York City. The airport was so huge that I became confused, and I panicked. I didn't understand how and where I could make a phone call to Mr. Udo in Atlanta. I strolled around in the airport, making a window-shopping. Later, I asked where I could find a public phone to place a call. I found one, and I made a call that morning to Mr. Udo. He answered me and asked where I was calling him from. I disclosed it to him I was at New York International Airport. He asked why I decided to take a decision like that without letting him be aware of my plan. My answer to him was that if he had a pre-knowledge, perhaps he would have prevented me from going to America. Again, perhaps he would have further discouraged by articulating he had been in the United States for only a year, still living with his uncle. Notwithstanding, he was heading to work that morning, so he instructed me to take the next flight to Atlanta and that when I get there, I should stay in the airport till he came to fetch me after work. I did exactly as he instructed me to do.

While waiting for the next connection to Atlanta, an elderly black man walked up to me and asked whether I was a Nigerian. To his surprise, the answer was yes. We started discussing; he narrated how friendly he was with some Nigerian friends in Cleveland, Ohio, when he used to live there. He told me he was heading back to Boston, where he lives. He gave me the names and phone numbers of the few friends in Cleveland to call. He suggested that I should go over to Cleveland and meet with the people if staying in Atlanta didn't suit me. We departed from each other (again). He was heading to Boston, Massachusetts, while I was going to Atlanta, Georgia. My friend (Udo) came to pick me up and drove straight to his residence, a welcomed moment in the United States. As we were having fun, his uncle came to the house, and after a while, Mr. Udo did the introduction. At that point, I noticed the atmosphere in the house changed, and my friend signaled me the danger. Literally, he confirmed that I couldn't stay with them and that there was no room to accommodate me as well. This was his uncle's statement. Mr. Udo asked where else I could go in the United States. I told him that I preferred Cleveland, Ohio. I told him about the man from Boston I met at the airport. Going to Cleveland was a certainty, and on the following day, on Sunday, Mr. Udo took me to the Greyhound bus terminal, where I boarded a bus to Cleveland. He bought a one-way ticket and offered me a total sum of three hundred dollars for my upkeep in Cleveland. We embraced each other, and he left. He said I should call him when I reached my destination.

In Cleveland, Ohio, I arrived at an early hour on Sunday morning. I met a terrifying and precarious situation, a place where I had no idea what was in store. I didn't call any of those numbers. I waited a while, presuming the fellows might have gone to a church service. Later, I called one of the numbers, and someone answered. He asked who I was and how I got his name and number. I narrated to him the story that a fellow I met at the New York airport used to live in Cleveland before moving to Boston. At that juncture, he acknowledged the person was indeed his friend, before relocating to Boston in Massachusetts. In our telephone conversation, the person asked me to wait for him at the Greyhound bus station and told me that after the church service, he would come down and fetch me. I did exactly as instruct. He came as promised and fetched me and went straight to the meeting hall where Nigerians held their monthly meetings. The name of the organization was NOK. The name was coined out of an archaeological culture that was widespread from circa 900 BC (before Christ) to the second-century AD over what is now northern and central Nigeria. On our way there to the meeting hall, I didn't ask or say anything to him. He kept driving, and in my mind, I thought he was taking me to his residence, but I was wrong. We arrived at the meeting venue, and I observed that every person in the hall stared at me, perhaps wondering who I was. This gentleman didn't stay long. I saw him leaving after the discussion with the president of the association. He left and didn't come back to say good-bye to me. It was at that point I professed that the gist was in my favor. At the meeting, during the arising matter, my issue came up third on the agenda for discussion. The president introduced me to the audience, asked a few questions before he handed the microphone to me to address the audience myself. Although I didn't say much to them, I simply told them that I was stranded in Cleveland and that I needed assistance from them. They felt sympathetic to my ordeal. They assured me they would take good care of me. Toward the closing of the meeting, the president asked every person if he or she would like to volunteer to accommodate me in his/her house. Among them was a man named Mr. Abu Alli from Akron, Ohio, who raised his hand and accepted to give me the hospitality.

Basically, I stayed with him for quite a while. Often, I rode with him to several places, including Cleveland. I met Mr. John Onoliefo, a Director of Buckeye Area Development and Emmanuel Onunwo, East Cleveland Major, and the others. Three of these men were instrumental in finding me a job. My permanent work was at the RD's Seafood and Steakhouse, in Buckeye, Ohio, as a dishwasher, and I often worked in the kitchen. Two dollars and a quarter were my hourly pay. The owner paid me under the table; I didn't have a green card or a work permit in the country. Every day, I commuted from Akron to Cleveland to work. Night shifts I worked, and when I didn't work, I visited friends. Most of the time, Mr. Abu Alli would allow me to drive his car without a driver's license. I was involved in a motor accident, and a case was filed for my driving without a license. I paid a fine, and I thought the case was over; however, unknowingly, Mr. Alli and I were both sued for one hundred thousand dollars each by the other driver. I didn't understand the implication of the lawsuit here in America; therefore, I overlooked, not till I looked at my credit report did I realize what took place. The moment I found out I decided not to act because I was new in town, and I didn't have any money to make a payment-arrangement plan with the fellow involved in the accident.

Obviously, I was advised I could get rid of it if I should file a chapter 7 bankruptcy. Mr. Alli arranged for me to meet some women. Among them, I chose one and made her my wife. We both lived together in the same apartment. My life began to shape differently, and I had a second job working as a security officer at the Central Control Security Company. The job didn't last long due to my negligence. My boss caught me sleeping on the job. My girlfriend usually dropped by and picked me up from work. There was an evidence that working at night in the restaurant caused my security job. Therefore, I was careful about what I did so that such trouble never again occurred. In December 1989, I married a girlfriend. My work pattern didn't change much. I continued to work illegally at the restaurant. Since I was married, I filed a petition for a change of status with the United States Immigration Office, sought a change from a visiting to a permanent residency. My wish was granted; however, there were prices I had to pay along to procure a green card. I had a second job working at the PSI Institute of Cleveland as a student recruiter. On the job, I didn't last long.

In 1989, I assisted in forming Nigerian Community in Greater Cleveland (NCGC). This was a nonprofit organization for all Nigerians, irrespective of their religion, ethnicity, and gender. The post of provost was bestowed upon me, which I performed diligently, to the best of my ability. In the cultural dance group, I was a key member, and in the Nigerian Independence

Day celebration, I joined on the stage performance. The group was a powerful group to be reckoned with in the Greater Cleveland area and beyond. When I left the organization after the end of my tenure, there was about thirty thousand dollars left in the bank account. The plan was to raise enough money to purchase our own building; however, the plan didn't work. At the same time, we established a Nigerian Charitable Fund (NCF) account that was to be used for the purpose stated above. The idea was to enhance our fund-raising ability. This meant that able people can freely denote money and write it off on their taxes at the end of the year. The whole purpose was defeated by some so-called Nigerian professionals who came in full force with their agenda and changed the name from the Nigerian Charitable Fund to National Charitable Fund. The idea didn't sit well with most of the members and didn't conform to the NCGC constitution. Due to the behaviors generated by some of our professionals, we decided to seek the aid of an attorney to pursue the case to the last logical conclusion against those behind the feign. Our side was victorious in the end. The name was changed back to the original name (Nigerian Charitable Fund). After the incident, there have been many problems never imagined before. The affected members of the lawsuit had abhorred our group, and as a result, splinter groups such as Yoruba Agbaropo Group, Edo Group, and Nzuko Ndi Ibo Group came. The organization became less effective and attractive, and many members withdrew their membership and stopped attending the meetings and other functions.

Akron University was where I registered to study mass communication at the master's level. I discontinued going there because I didn't have the financial ability to continue. At the same time, I registered also at Cuyahoga Community College– Metro Campus for a computer training course. All other activities were on hold till further notice. This was the reason that I was having some serious problems in my marriage; my wife had a personal problem. She spent carelessly, which obviously impacted our financial ability. She was helped to overcome her spending habit. She had also another serious problem, in my power, I tried everything possible, signed her up for the counseling center; nonetheless, it didn't help her much. Many friends suggested I should leave her alone because it would be impossible for her to change her ways. In fact, I wasn't keen on heeding their advice or suggestions. All I cared about and believed was, she would be helped by my effort.

The wonders started to surface when she was pregnant with our first child. She used illicit drugs at the time, the doctor advised her to quit doing it for the baby's good health. She did stop, as the doctor told her. When the baby came, I became busier, working long hours to support both the mom and the child. I had several temporary assignments, including the distribution of the *Plain Dealer* newspaper, *USA Today*, and *Telephone Directory* for residential homes and businesses. I took a job with the JB Medals Company Corp. (Berea, Ohio), worked as a press operator. Later, my wife joined the company. After a few months, I left the job for another, while my wife was still working there. I worked at the Plastic Piping System Inc. (Independence, Ohio), as a shipping/receiving manager, also managed a warehouse department. I stayed on the job for a while until another opportunity came from the Great Power Products Inc. (Mentor, Ohio), did the same assignment as a shipper and the warehouse person. I was with the company till I gathered enough money and the requirements to start my own transportation company. I started buying and kept things I would need to run the business, such as a cargo van, fax machine, typewriter, and other necessary items. The idea was discussed with my wife about my intention; however, she refused to see reason with me. Her objection was, I would spend a lot of money that we didn't have for the business purpose, and there was no guarantee I would be successful. I listened to her opinion, but I didn't take it seriously. I knew how much I was paying out to the trucking company in my job. I stood firm and, in my conviction, so I moved ahead with the business proposal. I created a space in my house and used it as a temporary office. A business phone line was installed; a part-time driver was hired. I printed some flyers, business cards, created a company website, and paid someone to act as a sales representative. The speed in which the business took off was very encouraging. I had a handful of customers before I decided to give a two-week quit notice to my job. At last and after two weeks ended, I stopped going to work and concentrated on mine.

I launched the company in January 1996. On-Time Delivery Services, Inc. was an official name and registered as a small corporation in the state of Ohio. It has a full operating authority in the states and beyond. In the business, I couldn't have a greater percentage share since I wasn't a US citizen. Only I had a permanent green card. Every document carried my wife's signature. An office space was rented; the operation was moved from my house to the new office. More staff members were added to the company's effectiveness. I did extremely great, and more office space was created to accommodate over fifteen staff members. At this or that juncture, my wife decided to quit her own job and joined to run On-Time Delivery Services. Mr. Charles Alatise became a partner in the business, invested ($50,000.00) fifty thousand dollars. He relocated to Wickliffe, Ohio, from Baltimore, Maryland. We worked together for a couple of days. Things didn't work out for both of us; therefore, I asked him to withdraw his partnership while necessary arrangement would be made to pay him back his money. Some of the money was paid back to him before the company filed chapter 11 bankruptcy. Also, a subsidiary company was added to the primary business. Budget Truck Rental had two locations, one in Euclid, Ohio and the other in Wickliffe, Ohio. My permanent resident status changed. I became a US citizen.

I filed for a divorce, and it was granted in 2002. I was still managing my businesses when I went to further my education. I earned a degree in Master of Business Administration (MBA) at the University of Phoenix–Cleveland Campus in 2003. In 2012, On-Time Delivery Services and its partner company came to a close when we lost the major accounts with the General Electric Company and others. This was due to the global economic meltdown, everyone was facing some years back. Almost every company got or get hit, particularly smaller businesses, the hardest. Furthermore, in 2014, I earned my doctorate from the University of the Rockies, Denver, Colorado, specializing in executive coaching, organizational leadership. Presently, I have both Zoom Logistics Inc., (Established, 2011), while the Reliance Coaching & Consulting (Established, 2011).

CHAPTER 5
CONCLUSION

I n conclusion, this autobiography has explained the efficacy of my dream, goal, and the success. Indeed, it has also explained where and how it all began some decades ago. Understanding the imperative, therefore, a dream does translate to reality if carefully analyzed and implemented. A dream can manifest in a series of images, ideas, emotions, and sensations that occur involuntarily in the mind during certain stages when a person is sleeping. My dream has played a vital role in my life that created a sense of urgency to trail the path to success. With respect to my goal, this has also played a key part of my success. This has helped create a commitment and drives plans and feedback.

Obviously, this is the bedrock that endeavored me to reach a finite time placed by a deadline. My goal emanated from the conscious decision-making process. The success has always been the ultimate achievement I dream for in life. The mission has been accomplished, and I have turned impossibility into a possibility. My success is audacious of my hope.

From the beginning to the end of my journey, I worked tirelessly to accomplish my goal. I envisioned, planned, and committed to achieving it. This was my personal desire, an end point in the expected development. I didn't wait to have a parent, uncles, relatives, and any good Samaritans to send me to school. I did it solely by putting more effort, zeal, tenacity, and hard work. I did it, and I believe anyone can do it too.

Finally, this autobiography is to show the readers that anything in life is possible. A person needs to just work harder and keep hope alive, and for sure, he or she will get there.